Daily Prayer

Pursuing Holiness

Daily Prayer

Pursuing Holiness

Berenice Aguilera

For my Church

Table of Contents

Introduction..1
My soul thirsts for you...5
The Lord He is God!...7
The Lord Almighty is with us................................9
Majestic in holiness..11
From death to life...13
You shall be holy, because I am holy...................15
Resting in God..17
His kingdom rules over all....................................19
Sealed and anointed..21
A place of abundance...23
Sing, O daughter of Zion!....................................25
How majestic is your name..................................27
Children of God...29
Predestined to an inheritance..............................31
Nothing will separate us from the love of God....33
Love the Lord your God...37
Faith not sight..39
Let the peace of Christ rule..................................41
They will be His people...43
Great and precious promises...............................45
Sing praises to God..47
Blessed are those who seek Him.........................49
My thoughts are not your thoughts.....................51

Like a tree planted by streams..............................53
Grace to persevere...55
Take my life..57
We are all the work of your hand..........................59
His compassion never fails....................................62
Be strong in the Lord..64
Holy, holy, holy is the Lord Almighty..................67
What's next?..69

Introduction

Pursuing Holiness, seems like a tall order, doesn't it?

How can we set our minds to this high calling, when we find it difficult to get down on our knees and worship and pray? You know, those times when you just feel apathetic about your faith, and maybe just too plain tired to talk to anyone, even God?

Here's an idea… and it works every time.

Just do it!

Yes!

JUST. DO. IT.

There is no waiting for the 'right time,' to pray, or seek God. The 'right time,' is always now!

Tell yourself, "Stop what you are doing and go and pray… now!" and just do it.

Talking to yourself, and telling yourself what to do is not an original idea.

King David did it. So if it's OK for him to do, it is certainly OK for the rest of us!

Take a look at Psalm 103. It is a Psalm full of David telling himself what to do.

If you break it down, it gives us loads of reasons to start our conversation with God straight away.

We are told to remember:

- All His benefits
- His forgiveness, and healing hand
- His redemptive power in your life
- The hope He gives you
- What He has done for you in the past
- His love and compassion
- The word He has planted in you
- His great and precious promises

And much more!

Our call as people of God, is one of holiness and perseverance. But this is impossible without the word and prayer being of first importance in our lives.

The first commandment, you shall have no other gods before me, is a hopeless dream, unless we renew our minds and seek His face.

The wisdom of Psalm 103 is that as we *think* of these things, our thinking is turned towards the goodness of God, and from there it is easy to worship and praise Him.

Sometimes we can be our own worst enemy when it comes to seeking God. We want the *quiet time*, or a*lone time.* The *ideal* condition for seeking God. For most of us, we manage it for a few days, weeks even, but inevitably *life* can get in the way.

I have found it really helpful in remembering our life with God is a 24 hour walk. Not a half hour meeting or interview. Whilst those *alone time*s can be wonderful, our remembering His benefits, or forgiveness, or any number of His blessings, can be done any time in the day. And as we fill our thoughts with Him, the Holy Spirit directs our hearts in worship and petition.

Pursuing holiness doesn't make us better than the next person, or earn points with God. We pursue holiness because we seek after God. We seek to please Him and draw close to Him, and love Him more today than we did yesterday.

So take heart my dear brother, my dear sister. As

you read the following pages, through Scripture, and prayer, know that He is at work in your heart and life, drawing you to Him, and molding you into the image of His precious Son.

My soul thirsts for you

Psalm 63:1

O God, you are my God! I long for you!
My soul thirsts for you, my flesh yearns
for you, in a dry and parched land where
there is no water.

O God, you alone know how I long for you. You know how I long for holiness and complete obedience to your will. I know it is you who has given me those desires. I know that no such desire can come from my own will.

Lord I long for the day where the corruption of indwelling sin is destroyed completely, at the coming of your Son Jesus. But until that day, I ask that you would continue to give me grace to overcome sin, especially spiritual pride.

O God, make me more like you. Give me desire to live more for you. Help me never to be content with the little I know of your word. Grant that I might always desire to know more and do more.

Wrap my life in your divine love, and keep me ever desiring you. Grant me a truly humble heart, completely given over to your will, so that I might walk in obedience to you every day of my life. I ask in Jesus name, amen.

Further reading - 1 John 3 / Psalm 51

The Lord He is God!

1 Kings 18:36-39

*At the time of sacrifice, the prophet
Elijah stepped forward and prayed:
"Lord, the God of Abraham, Isaac and
Israel, let it be known today that you are
God in Israel and that I am your servant
and have done all these things at your
command.*

*Answer me, Lord, answer me, so these
people will know that you, Lord, are
God, and that you are turning their
hearts back again."*

*Then the fire of the Lord fell and burned
up the sacrifice, the wood, the stones
and the soil, and also licked up the water
in the trench.*

*When all the people saw this, they fell
prostrate and cried, "The Lord—he is
God! The Lord—he is God!"*

Father, help me to worship you with my life, not just my words. I think of Elijah's water-soaked sacrifice and how fire came down and completely consumed it, water and all. I want my life to be like this. Totally consumed by your power, and wholly belonging to you. Give me grace to overcome the desires of my heart that are ungodly. Help me choose to obey you and put to death every evil thought.

O God, you are the great heart turner. When you touched my life, your mercy was poured upon me and you created in me a completely new heart. You gave me power over sin, and my own selfish desires. Without your work in my life, I know it is impossible to please you.

Grant that I might desire what you desire. Grant that I might truly be a living sacrifice, dedicated wholly to your service. Sanctify me, O Lord. Purify my heart. Renew my mind by the power of your word. I ask all this in your holy name, Jesus. Amen.

Further reading - Ezekiel 36:22-38 / Hebrews 10

The Lord Almighty is with us
Psalm 46:4-7

There is a river whose streams make glad the city of God, the holy place where the Most High dwells. God is within her, she will not fall; God will help her at break of day. Nations are in uproar, kingdoms fall; he lifts his voice, the earth melts. The Lord Almighty is with us; the God of Jacob is our fortress.

O Lord my God, I worship you. I can't begin to find the words to say how much I love you.

I love you for your mercy and grace. I love you for your goodness and purity, your justice and your holiness. I love you for you have changed my heart so I can truly proclaim, that though the nations are in uproar, and kingdoms fall, you alone are the fortress of your people, in you alone is safety.

O God, I long to be made holy, as you are holy. I

long for the day when every impurity in my life will be gone forever. Every wrong thought, every wrong deed, all gone for eternity. I long to see your face and be in your presence forever.

Thank you for your forgiveness. Thank you that you have reconciled me to you by the death of your precious son Jesus. I have been delivered from the power of sin, and I am so grateful.

Purify my heart, O Lord. Purify my mind and deeds. If I need to be put through trials in order to refine me like gold, let your will be done. Give me grace to overcome temptation, and lead me so that I will never be overwhelmed by evil.

Give me love for your people. Give me love for the guilty world that will cause me to proclaim your gospel to them.

I ask in Jesus name, amen.

Further reading – Revelation 4 / 2 Corinthians 5

Majestic in holiness

Exodus 15:11

Who among the gods is like you, Lord?
Who is like you — majestic in holiness,
awesome in glory, working wonders?

You are worthy of all adoration and glory, for you alone are holy, O Lord. Your name is above every name, your goodness and love, no-one can comprehend. You are so high above all, your beauty, so precious, who can understand you? Your love is higher than the heavens, your faithfulness reaches to the skies. Your righteousness is like the highest mountains, and your justice like the ocean deep. You, O Lord, preserve both people and animals. How priceless is your unfailing love, O God.

Your people take refuge in the shadow of your wings. They feast on the abundance of your house;

you give them drink from your river of delights. For with you is the fountain of life; in your light we see light. Continue your love to those who know you, your righteousness to the upright in heart.

Sanctify me, O Lord, spirit, soul, and body. Grant that above all things, I will love your word. Grant that I would see more of you, as I read, listen, and learn. Give me strength to overcome sin. O Lord, be my strength and shield. May I never let sin rest in me. Give me grace always to recognise it, and to repent and turn away.

As difficulties come, grant me grace to walk through them without fear. Draw me near to you, and make me holy. I know that you have begun your good work in me, and that you will carry it out til the end. You will work in my heart to both will, and carry out your own good pleasure.

Thank you O Lord, for your work in my life. Amen.

Further reading - Psalm 36:5-10 / 1 Kings 8

From death to life

Romans 6:11-14

*So you also must consider yourselves dead
to sin and alive to God in Christ Jesus. Let
not sin therefore reign in your mortal body,
to make you obey its passions. Do not
present your members to sin as instruments
for unrighteousness, but present yourselves
to God as those who have been brought
from death to life, and your members to
God as instruments for righteousness. For
sin will have no dominion over you, since
you are not under law but under grace.*

O Lord my God, I confess that all things come from
you; life, breath, happiness, sight, touch, hearing,
truth, love… everything that makes our lives good.

I know that I am entirely dependent on you. I ask
for grace to know more of my need of grace. O
God, I pray you would forgive my sins. Forgive me
for not honouring you as you should be honoured.

13

Forgive me for often not putting you first, or even thinking about you when making decisions. Forgive me for my neglect of your word, and seeking to know you.

Show me my sin, so that I might confess and repent. Thank you for each time you grant me repentance. I know that the desire to do so comes ONLY from you.

Forgive me for the times I have asked forgiveness without real thought. I ask that I might confess my sin with deep mourning and regret, and a deep understanding of how I have disobeyed you. Let there be no pretence, or 'glossing over,' what I have done. Let there be no minimising of wrongdoing. The price that was paid to cleanse me of sin was high. Let me never forget.

Let me always walk in the light of the shed blood of your beloved Son. Let me never take it lightly. O God, forgive me the times I have done so. Let my heart be resolved to know nothing, but Jesus Christ, and Him crucified. Amdn.

Further reading - Eph 4:17-32 / Psalm 32

You shall be holy, because I am holy.

1 Peter 1:13-16

Therefore, get your minds ready for action by being fully sober, and set your hope completely on the grace that will be brought to you when Jesus Christ is revealed. Like obedient children, do not comply with the evil urges you used to follow in your ignorance, but, like the Holy One who called you, become holy yourselves in all of your conduct, for it is written, "You shall be holy, because I am holy."

My God, it would be heaven to perfectly please you, and be all what you would have me be. O that I would be holy as you are holy, pure as Christ is pure, and perfect as your Spirit is perfect.

How easy I find it to break your law. I want to do what is right, but I find myself not doing it. I do the very thing I was determined not to do. I so delight in your word with all my heart, yet I find myself so easily turned aside from it. How can I live this way, when you are infinite in goodness and grace towards me?

I cry with the apostle Paul, "Who will rescue me from this body of death? Thanks be to God through Jesus Christ our Lord!"

You are rich in mercy. Washing away the sins of those who belong to you, and declaring them righteous. Because of my precious Saviour, Jesus Christ, I can stand before you, a child beloved by her Father.

Amazing grace, how sweet the sound that saved a wretch like me!

My true hope is set on the grace that will be brought to me when Jesus Christ is revealed. O for that day to be soon!

O God of grace, grant me the heart and mind to turn away from sin. I want to be holy in all of my thoughts and actions, for your name's sake, amen.

Further reading - Romans chapters 7 and 8

Resting in God

Matthew 11:28-30

Come to me, all you who are weary and burdened, and I will give you rest. Take my yoke on you and learn from me, because I am gentle and humble in heart, and you will find rest for your souls. For my yoke is easy to bear, and my load is not hard to carry.

O God, the thought of your infinite peace lifts my heart. Whilst I toil, and strive, and work, and struggle, you are forever at perfect peace. O God, I look to you, my Redeemer, my Strength and my Song. Your power knows no bounds. My every defeat, you turn into victory. The Lord Almighty reigns!

Create deep faith in my heart. Let me always seek to draw close to you, my heavenly Shepherd. Let me to hear your voice, and obey. Keep me from

17

deception by causing me to abide in your word. Keep me from harm by helping me walk in the power of the Spirit.

Grant me deep roots into your eternal truths, so that I might walk in them. Let me never be ashamed of the truth of the gospel, no matter the situation.

Lord help me, for I am often lukewarm, even cold. Unbelief creeps in, and sin makes me forget you. Help me to always remember that I only truly live, when I live to you. Your presence alone can make me holy, faithful, strong and joyful. Abide in me, O gracious God, in Jesus name I pray, amen.

Further reading - Titus 2:11-14 / Revelation 3:14-22

His kingdom rules over all
Psalm 103:17-19

But the steadfast love of the Lord is from everlasting to everlasting on those who fear him, and his righteousness to children's children, to those who keep his covenant and remember to do his commandments. The Lord has established his throne in the heavens, and his kingdom rules over all.

O God of my beginning, and God of my end, you are from everlasting to everlasting. Your kingdom rules over all, and all will one day bow before you. The heart of man will plan a way, but it is your purposes that will prevail. Nothing can stand against your will, and your plan for every life. You are truly Sovereign.

It is my delight to think on such things. My heart revels in your power and your glory, and with all my being I long for you.

I long to know you more, with both my heart, and my mind. I want to spend each day pursuing you, and submit to you as you work in my life, changing me to conform to your will. It is my joy to see your grace being revealed.

O God, change my heart so I might be steadfast in my love for you. Change me so that I might have you constantly in view, looking neither to the right or to the left. I ask that distractions I may once have longed for, may become nothing, compared to the desire to know you more.

I long to fill my time with you, whether at home or away; to place all my worries in your hands, and be completely at your disposal, having no interest or desire for my own way.

These are the things my heart longs for, yet seem so far away. There is so much that must be changed!

Help me to live for you, forever; to make you and your glory my motivation for living, so that I may never put my will over yours. I ask this in the name of Jesus Christ, my Lord and Saviour, Amen.

Further reading - Prov 4:20-27 / Prov 16:1-3

Sealed and anointed

2 Corinthians 1:18-22

As surely as God is faithful, our word to you has not been Yes and No. For the Son of God, Jesus Christ, whom we proclaimed among you... was not Yes and No, but in him it is always Yes. For all the promises of God find their Yes in him. That is why it is through him that we utter our Amen to God for his glory. And it is God who establishes us with you in Christ, and has anointed us, and who has also put his seal on us and given us his Spirit in our hearts as a guarantee.

O Lord, my God, all your promises in Christ Jesus are yes and amen, and every one of them will be fulfilled. You have spoken, and they will be done. You have commanded, and they will come to pass.

Yet I have often doubted you, and lived as if there

were no God. I have found significance in something other than you, and been content with worldly interests.

But because of your great grace towards me, I have repented. I trust in you. I trust your words. I trust your plans.

Teach me to submit to your will, to delight in your laws, and to truly believe that everything you do is for my good. Help me to leave my worries in your hands, for you alone have the power to direct events around me. Help me to trust you, as your plans and purposes come to pass in my life.

Bless me with a faith like Abraham's, that didn't stumble with unbelief at your promises.

I ask that I might be faithful to you through trials. Help me to see beyond those trials to your glory.

O God, I am so far away from being the kind of person I want to be. I am so far from reflecting the goodness and grace of your Son. Soften my heart and mould me into a vessel for your honour. For without you working miracles in me to change my fickle heart, I know there is no hope.

I ask this in Jesus name, amen

Further reading - Romans 12 / Ephesians 2:1-10

A place of abundance

Psalm 66:8-12

Bless our God, O peoples; let the sound of his praise be heard, who has kept our soul among the living and has not let our feet slip.

For you, O God, have tested us; you have tried us as silver is tried. You brought us into the net; you laid a crushing burden on our backs; you let men ride over our heads; we went through fire and through water; yet you have brought us out to a place of abundance.

Lord of eternity, before whom angels bow and archangels veil their faces, help me to serve you with reverence and godly fear.

You are truly God, and require truth in the inward parts. Help me to worship you in spirit and in truth.

23

You are truly righteous. Let me not harbour sin in my heart, or indulge in worldly passions, or seek satisfaction in things that perish.

I ask that you would mold me so that earthly pursuits and possessions would be meaningless. That whether rich or poor, successful or unsuccessful, admired or despised, all I would know, or want to know, is your faithfulness and mercy. All I would care about is hungering and thirsting after righteousness, and loving you with all my heart.

Grant that these desires might produce good works. Form in me all those principles and desires that make serving you, perfect freedom.

Rid my mind of all sinful fear and shame, so that with firmness and courage I might confess you before all men. Give me grace to bear persecution for your sake. Give me godly wisdom, and zeal. Grant that I might remember to consult you on all things, and seek Scripture to know your will.

O Lord, give me that perfect peace only you can give, knowing that nothing can befall me without your permission, your decision, or your direction.

Thank you for your constant faithfulness towards your people, in Jesus name, amen.

Further reading - Matthew 5:6-25 / Isaiah 26:3-4

Sing, O daughter of Zion!

Zephaniah 3:14-17

Sing aloud, O daughter of Zion; shout, O Israel! Rejoice and exult with all your heart, O daughter of Jerusalem!

The Lord has taken away the judgments against you; he has cleared away your enemies.

The King of Israel, the Lord, is in your midst; you shall never again fear evil.

On that day it shall be said to Jerusalem: "Fear not, O Zion; let not your hands grow weak.

The Lord your God is in your midst, a mighty one who will save; he will rejoice over you with gladness; he will quiet you by his love; he will exult over you with loud singing.

O God of our Lord Jesus Christ, you are the light of my salvation, and the delight of my soul. Your word says that you rejoice over your people with gladness, you will quiet us with your love, and exult over us with loud singing! What joy there is in your presence! What wonder there is in your love!

We who were once your enemies, you have made sons and daughters. You have removed judgement from us, and the fear of death we once had, you have removed far from us. Never again will we fear the future. Never again will we be filled with terror at facing you.

O God, you are mighty in our midst. In you, and you alone is there salvation. By your grace, I am free. By your mercy I am redeemed, and my sins forgiven. May your Spirit draw me nearer to you and your ways.

Let my life be lived by your holy word, and make your commandments the joy of my heart. May I ever grow in your love and in turn show it to those living around me.

O Holy Spirit, make me love like Jesus. Grant me goodness of heart, and a willingness to obey your word, so that my life might shine before men to the praise of your glory. I ask you to humble my heart. Give me grace to become meek, like my Saviour, and always ready to give you honour. Amen

Further reading - Psalm 27 / Romans 5

How majestic is your name

Psalm 8:3-9

*When I look at your heavens, the work of
your fingers, the moon and the stars,
which you have set in place, what is man
that you are mindful of him, and the son
of man that you care for him?*

*Yet you have made him a little lower
than the heavenly beings and crowned
him with glory and honor.*

*You have given him dominion over the
works of your hands; you have put all
things under his feet, all sheep and oxen,
and also the beasts of the field, the birds
of the heavens, and the fish of the sea,
whatever passes along the paths of the
seas.*

*O Lord, our Lord, how majestic is your
name in all the earth!*

O Lord, my God, you are the Maker and Sustainer

of all things. Day and night belong to you; the heavens and earth declare your glory. What is man that you are mindful of him? The son of man that you care for him? You have taken from your enemies, and made for yourself a chosen people, a royal priesthood, a holy nation. What glory! What wonder, it is to be one of those chosen!

Once we did not receive mercy, but now we have received mercy. O God, give us grace to overcome temptation. Help us to live according to your word, so that we might proclaim your goodness to all men. You who have called us out of darkness, into your marvellous light, give us grace to live according to your will.

Deliver me from worldly longings, for I am born from above, and am heaven-bound. Let me never grow apathetic, or lose the assurance of my salvation. Equip me for every circumstance you bring me into.

Help me always to think and draw strength from you. Turn my trials into blessings, so that my heart might be filled with gratitude and praise, as I see their design and effects.

Give me grace to be content in all things, I ask in Jesus holy name, amen.

Further reading - 1 Peter 2 / Hebrews 13

Children of God

Philippians 2:12-16

Therefore, my beloved, as you have always obeyed, so now, not only as in my presence but much more in my absence, work out your own salvation with fear and trembling, for it is God who works in you, both to will and to work for his good pleasure.

Do all things without grumbling or disputing, that you may be blameless and innocent, children of God without blemish in the midst of a crooked and twisted generation, among whom you shine as lights in the world, holding fast to the word of life...

O God, full of grace and mercy. I worship you, for you alone are worthy of all honour and glory. May your name be blessed for ever and ever.

Teach me to live by prayer. Give me words to

worship and praise you. Give me words to pray for my family, my church and my neighbours. O God, guide me by your Holy Spirit to pray according to your will. I pray you will sanctify me. Let my heart, my character and my thoughts reflect your holiness. Keep me from evil, and the temptation of my own desires.

Let me truly know that the work of prayer is to bring my will in line with yours, and without this knowledge, all I will end up praying is my will and my own selfish desires. And I don't want that.

Grant me wisdom to live a godly life and make godly choices. I want love to be formed in my heart. True, holy, godly love. A love like yours, that is so full of grace, and patience, and joy. Change my heart, O God. I am so far from the holiness of life that I seek. Work in me to will and to do your good purpose.

How is it that I grumble and complain? How is it that I forget the work my beloved Saviour has done for me? O God, forgive me. Give me grace to live a life that shines in the darkness.

O God, let your name be glorified. Let your kingdom come and your will be done, always.

In Jesus name, amen.

Further reading - Matthew 26:36-46 / Ephesians 5

Predestined to an inheritance

Ephesians 1:11-14

*In him we have obtained an inheritance,
having been predestined according to the
purpose of him who works all things
according to the counsel of his will, so
that we who were the first to hope in
Christ might be to the praise of his glory.
In him you also, when you heard the
word of truth, the gospel of your
salvation, and believed in him, were
sealed with the promised Holy Spirit,
who is the guarantee of our inheritance
until we acquire possession of it, to the
praise of his glory.*

Lord God Almighty, I am truly blessed to belong to
you. I am truly blessed that you chose to reveal
your Son to me, in all His humility and majesty, and
grace and glory.

I continually think on the fact that you reached into

31

the darkness and brought me into your kingdom of light. I am less than nothing. Yet you knew me. You chose me. You wrote my name in your book, and have given me eternal life. How wonderful are your ways, O God. How awe inspiring your work amongst your people.

O, that I might live according to your will. I long for the day when I will no longer struggle with sin. No longer will there be tears, or sorrow, or pain. I long for the day to see my Saviour's face, so full of joy in His bride. What a day that will be!

O God, you are holy. You have called your people, to be a holy people. And I want this in my life.

God, with all my heart I want to be changed. I want my every thought, and desire and action to bring glory to you, whether it is seen by others or not. It doesn't matter. You see me. And that is all that counts.

Lord, I honour you. I praise your glorious grace. Amen.

Further reading - Colossians 1:9-14 / Malachi 3:16-18

Nothing will separate us from the love of God

Rom 8:26-39

Likewise the Spirit also helps in our weaknesses. For we do not know what we should pray for as we ought, but the Spirit Himself makes intercession for us with groanings which cannot be uttered.

Now He who searches the hearts knows what the mind of the Spirit is, because He makes intercession for the saints according to the will of God.

And we know that all things work together for good to those who love God, to those who are the called according to His purpose.

For whom He foreknew, He also predestined to be conformed to the image of His Son, that He might be the firstborn among many brethren.

Moreover whom He predestined, these He also called; whom He called, these

He also justified; and whom He justified, these He also glorified.

What then shall we say to these things? If God is for us, who can be against us? He who did not spare His own Son, but delivered Him up for us all, how shall He not with Him also freely give us all things?

Who shall bring a charge against God's elect? It is God who justifies. Who is he who condemns?

It is Christ who died, and furthermore is also risen, who is even at the right hand of God, who also makes intercession for us. Who shall separate us from the love of Christ? Shall tribulation, or distress, or persecution, or famine, or nakedness, or peril, or sword? As it is written:

"For Your sake we are killed all day long; We are accounted as sheep for the slaughter."

Yet in all these things we are more than conquerors through Him who loved us.

For I am persuaded that neither death nor life, nor angels nor principalities nor powers, nor things present nor things to come, nor height nor depth, nor any other created thing, shall be able to separate us from the love of God which is in Christ Jesus our Lord.

Lord God, heavenly King, what favour, what mercy there is to be under your constant guidance and care. What joy there is in being in the presence of your word! I ask that you would guide me when times are difficult.

When things are difficult, I ask that you would use those difficulties to brighten my heart, and grow my faith, so I might not dishonour you. Help me to wait patiently for your guidance.

Let me never lose heart, or sight of the fact, that you will never let me go. I know that nothing can separate me from your love.

Neither angels or demons, neither the present nor the future, nor any powers, neither height nor depth, nor anything else in all creation will be able to separate those who belong to you, from the love of God that is in Christ Jesus, my Lord and my God.

What precious comfort and peace there is in knowing you.

[1]Take my heart and hold it in thy hand; write upon it reverence to thyself with an inscription that time and eternity cannot erase. To thy grace and the care of thy covenant I commit myself, in sickness, and in health, for thou hast overcome the world.

You are truly God over all. May all honour and glory be ascribed to your name, now and always, amen.

Further reading - Isaiah 41:10 / Isaiah 42:16
[1]The Valley of Vision

Love the Lord your God

Deuteronomy 6:4-9

"Hear, O Israel: The Lord our God, the Lord is one! You shall love the Lord your God with all your heart, with all your soul, and with all your strength.

"And these words which I command you today shall be in your heart. You shall teach them diligently to your children, and shall talk of them when you sit in your house, when you walk by the way, when you lie down, and when you rise up. You shall bind them as a sign on your hand, and they shall be as frontlets between your eyes. You shall write them on the doorposts of your house and on your gates.

Truly you, O Lord, are worthy of all honour, and glory, and power, and praise. For your name is above every name. At the name of Jesus, every knee will bow, every tongue confess that you are Lord. Let praises resound in the earth! Let every living being declare your glory, for you created all things, and all things are subject to you.

O holy God, my heart is filled with longing for you. I long for the day when I will see you face to face, and be in your presence always. I long to stand in the congregation of the saints and of the angels, and sing your praises. O God, I wish I had words to express my love for you. My devotion to your name. All I know is that this yearning comes from you. My love and growing hunger for your presence are all a work of your Holy Spirit in my life. I know that. And I want more!

O Lord, grant me a heart that will hold more love for you. A mind that will hold more knowledge of you. And strength, that I might do every good work you put before me. I ask in Jesus name, amen.

Further reading - Philippians 2:1-16 / Revelation 7:9-17

Faith not sight

2 Corinthians 5:1-7

For we know that if our earthly house, this tent, is destroyed, we have a building from God, a house not made with hands, eternal in the heavens.

For in this we groan, earnestly desiring to be clothed with our habitation which is from heaven, if indeed, having been clothed, we shall not be found naked.

For we who are in this tent groan, being burdened, not because we want to be unclothed, but further clothed, that mortality may be swallowed up by life.

Now He who has prepared us for this very thing is God, who also has given us the Spirit as a guarantee.

So we are always confident, knowing that while we are at home in the body we are absent from the Lord. For we walk by faith, not by sight.

Lord Jesus, you said to consider the ravens, who neither sow or reap. And to consider the lilies how they grow, and spin not. O God you provide for your creation, so how much more will you provide for those whom you have chosen before the foundation of the world.

I want to walk by faith, and not by sight. No matter how things may appear, I know that you work all things for the good of those who love you, and are called according to your purpose. I know that whether I live through times of need, or times of plenty, you continue to work out your will in my life.

Thank you for all you give me. Let me never look to anyone else but you as my provider. Let me never raise up an idol in your place. You and you alone are the one who sustains life and provides for all you have made.

Soften my heart, O Lord, Give me faith to trust you implicitly. Open my understanding that I might know you more. Grant me wisdom to read your word and grow in knowledge. For the more I understand, the more I can grow in trusting you.

I ask this in Jesus name, amen.

Further reading - Luke 12:22-40 / Matthew 6:9-15

Let the peace of Christ rule

Colossians 3:12-17

Therefore, as God's chosen people, holy and dearly loved, clothe yourselves with compassion, kindness, humility, gentleness and patience. Bear with each other and forgive one another if any of you has a grievance against someone.

Forgive as the Lord forgave you. And over all these virtues put on love, which binds them all together in perfect unity.

Let the peace of Christ rule in your hearts, since as members of one body you were called to peace. And be thankful.

Let the message of Christ dwell among you richly as you teach and admonish one another with all wisdom through psalms, hymns, and songs from the Spirit, singing to God with gratitude in your hearts.

And whatever you do, whether in word

or deed, do it all in the name of the Lord
Jesus, giving thanks to God the Father
through him.

O God, how precious is your name. You alone are worthy to receive all honour, and power and glory and praise.

Sanctify me, O Lord. Send your Spirit to saturate my mind, overcome my every passion, and bring my nature in obedience to your word.

Come, Holy Spirit! I ask for perfect holiness, complete consecration, and entire cleansing from every evil. Take my heart, my head, my hands, my feet and use it all for your glory. Take my life, my family, my house, my belongings and use it for your service. Take my money and use it as you will. I bring any talent I might have and leave it at your feet. Use me as you will.

May my every breath be for you. Every minute spent for you. Let me be salt in the midst of my family, and work, and neighbourhood.

Now to the King eternal, immortal, invisible, the only God, be honour and glory for ever and ever. Amen.

Further reading - 2 Corinthians 7:1 / Matthew 13:44-46

They will be His people
Revelation 21:3-5

And I heard a loud voice from the throne saying, "Look! God's dwelling place is now among the people, and he will dwell with them. They will be his people, and God himself will be with them and be their God. 'He will wipe every tear from their eyes. There will be no more death' or mourning or crying or pain, for the old order of things has passed away."

He who was seated on the throne said, "I am making everything new!" Then he said, "Write this down, for these words are trustworthy and true."

Lord God, keep me from sin. Teach me to walk in holiness. Enable me to guard my mind against error of doctrine, my heart against wrong feelings, and my life against evil actions. Guard me against speaking unwisely, and giving way to anger. Keep me from idolatry.

I ask that my life would be one of grace and light. May your love live and reign in me. Help me not to live for myself, but to help provide for the needs of others. I want to live for you, with everything that entails. Grant me a Christ-like character, and may my life reflect the light we receive from Him.

O, how I long for you, my Lord and my Saviour. I long for the day when I will see you face to face. What joy there will be on that day! No more tears, or sadness. No more struggle against sin and evil. O God, may that day come soon!

But until that day, keep me in your paths. Guard my heart against all evil desires. Help me walk in humility and truth. I ask in Jesus name, amen.

Further reading - 1 Peter 1 / John 13:1-17

Great and precious promises
2 Peter 1:3-8

*His divine power has given us everything
we need for a godly life through our
knowledge of him who called us by his
own glory and goodness. Through these
he has given us his very great and
precious promises, so that through them
you may participate in the divine nature,
having escaped the corruption in the
world caused by evil desires.*

*For this very reason, make every effort to
add to your faith goodness; and to
goodness, knowledge; and to knowledge,
self-control; and to self-control,
perseverance; and to perseverance,
godliness; and to godliness, mutual
affection; and to mutual affection, love.
For if you possess these qualities in
increasing measure, they will keep you
from being ineffective and unproductive
in your knowledge of our Lord Jesus
Christ.*

O Lord, your divine power has granted me everything I need to live a life to please you. What an incredible truth! You give me EVERYTHING I need to live according to your word!

O God, let this truth permeate my heart. Let it work it's way through every thought, every desire, and every action. You have called me to your own glory and excellence. You have given me eternal life. What a precious gift you have given me. I am so grateful.

I know that adding any kind of goodness, or knowledge, or self control, or any of the qualities listed above, to my life is an absolute impossibility in my own strength. Yet the work of your Holy Spirit will accomplish all this. Let these beautiful characteristics grow in me as I live my life, so I might walk faithfully before you.

Thank you that you have broken the chains of sin in my life. Thank you that you have snatched me out of the corruption that sinful desire brings. Holy God, how great thou art! How wonderful are your deeds, O Lord God almighty. Let heaven and earth sing your praises, for you alone are worthy of all praise. Amen.

Further reading - John 15 / 2 Corinthians 9

Sing praises to God

Psalm 47: 1-9

Clap your hands, all you nations; shout to God with cries of joy. For the Lord Most High is awesome, the great King over all the earth.

He subdued nations under us, peoples under our feet. He chose our inheritance for us, pride of Jacob, whom he loved.

God has ascended amid shouts of joy, the Lord amid the sounding of trumpets.

Sing praises to God, sing praises; sing praises to our King, sing praises. For God is the King of all the earth; sing to him a psalm of praise.

God reigns over the nations; God is seated on his holy throne. The nobles of the nations assemble as the people of the God of Abraham, for the kings of the earth belong to God; he is greatly exalted.

Behold, God is my salvation: I will trust, and will not be afraid; for the Lord God is my strength and my song, and He has become my salvation. Give thanks to the Lord, call upon His name, make known His deeds among the peoples, and proclaim that His name is exalted.

Sing praises to the Lord, for He has done gloriously; let this be made known in all the earth. Shout, and sing for joy, O inhabitant of Zion, for great in your midst is the Holy One of Israel.

For the kings heart is in the hand of the Lord, like the rivers of water, He turns it wherever He wishes. For you are almighty, all powerful. None can stand against you.

You direct the heart of nations for your glory. Your strength is impossible to withstand. You raise up kingdoms, and you bring down empires according to your will. Nothing can stand against you.

You are our firm foundation. Our God in whom we trust. King of kings, and Lord of lords. You are our steadfast love, and our fortress, our stronghold and our deliverer, our shield and the One in whom we take refuge.

Glory be to the Father, and to the Son, and to the Holy Spirit, Amen.

Further reading - Isaiah 12:2-6 / Prov 21:1-2 / Psalm 144

Blessed are those who seek Him

Psalm 119:1-8

Blessed are those whose ways are blameless, who walk according to the law of the Lord. Blessed are those who keep his statutes and seek him with all their heart — they do no wrong but follow his ways.

You have laid down precepts that are to be fully obeyed.

Oh, that my ways were steadfast in obeying your decrees! Then I would not be put to shame when I consider all your commands.

I will praise you with an upright heart as I learn your righteous laws. I will obey your decrees; do not utterly forsake me.

Blessed are those whose ways are blameless, who walk in the law of the Lord! Blessed are those who keep his statutes and seek Him with all their heart, they do no wrong but follow his ways.

O God, I want my life to reflect these verses. I know you have cleansed my heart through Christ's precious blood shed on the cross. I know that you have given me His righteousness, and broken every chain of sin. I pray that I might be faithful to your word always. I ask you would grant me a heart that would seek you continually. I want to walk in your ways, in wisdom and truth.

Guard my heart O Lord. Protect me from temptations that threaten to overwhelm me. Give me grace to overcome, in Jesus name. Lead me always in paths of righteousness, and away from evil.

When I go through the valley of the shadow of death, remind me to lift up my head and see my Saviour. Let me not be crushed by circumstances, but instead walk in steadfast faith in the knowledge you are by my side, and will never leave me. You are always there to protect, guide and encourage.

Blessed be your holy name, Amen.

Further reading - 1 John 1 / Psalm 1

My thoughts are not your thoughts
Isaiah 55:8-9

For my thoughts are not your thoughts, neither are your ways my ways, declares the LORD. For as the heavens are higher than the earth, so are my ways higher than your ways and my thoughts than your thoughts.

For as the rain and the snow come down from heaven and do not return there but water the earth, making it bring forth and sprout, giving seed to the sower and bread to the eater, so shall my word be that goes out from my mouth; it shall not return to me empty, but it shall accomplish that which I purpose, and shall succeed in the thing for which I sent it

Lord God, you are above all. Your goodness and mercy know no end. Let your name be lifted up in the heavens, and let the earth resound with your

51

praise. For you are worthy of all power and glory, my King and my Lord.

Your word is powerful and accomplishes all your purposes. All your words succeed in the goal you meant them for.

O God, let your word dwell in me richly. Let your ways and thoughts mould all of my ways and thoughts. Change my innermost being to love you continually, and direct me in obedience always. Let your thoughts become my thoughts.

Lord, grant me understanding as I read your word. Let me be an encouragement to your people, and grant that I would be given words of hope and life to the lost. Let my first inclination always be to seek your word about circumstances I am in. I ask for wisdom to discern right from wrong.

O God, give me grace to live according to your will. What comfort there is in the fact that every word from your mouth accomplishes your purpose. No matter what is going on in my life, I am assured that you are working your purpose in me, and those around me.

Blessed be your holy name. Amen.

Further reading - James 1;19-27 / John 17

Like a tree planted by streams
Psalm 1:1-6

Blessed is the one who does not walk in step with the wicked or stand in the way that sinners take or sit in the company of mockers, but whose delight is in the law of the Lord, and who meditates on his law day and night. That person is like a tree planted by streams of water, which yields its fruit in season and whose leaf does not wither — whatever they do prospers.

Not so the wicked! They are like chaff that the wind blows away. Therefore the wicked will not stand in the judgment, nor sinners in the assembly of the righteous.

For the Lord watches over the way of the righteous, but the way of the wicked leads to destruction.

Holy God, let my life be rooted and grounded in

your love. Give me more understanding of your love toward us. Help me understand the meaning of the gospel, the cross, the resurrection. Open my mind to the depths of your truth and love.

O God, I want to understand more. Teach me. Open my ears that I might hear. Give me perseverance to study and seek out answers, so that I might know you more. Gift me with wisdom and knowledge, so that I might grow in maturity in my faith, and so that I might serve your body faithfully.

Lord God, I can't put in to words the longing I have for you. For your presence, and for knowledge of you.

Forgive me for often wasting my time when it could have been spent seeking you. Forgive me for my apathy and selfishness. O God, cleanse my heart, renew a right spirit within me. I ask that I might serve you faithfully all the days of my life, in Jesus name, amen.

Further reading - Ephesians 3 / 1 Corinthians 2

Grace to persevere

James 1:2-8; 12

*Consider it pure joy, my brothers and
sisters, whenever you face trials of many
kinds, because you know that the testing
of your faith produces perseverance. Let
perseverance finish its work so that you
may be mature and complete, not lacking
anything. If any of you lacks wisdom,
you should ask God, who gives
generously to all without finding fault,
and it will be given to you. But when you
ask, you must believe and not doubt,
because the one who doubts is like a
wave of the sea, blown and tossed by the
wind. That person should not expect to
receive anything from the Lord. Such a
person is double-minded and unstable in
all they do.*

*Blessed is the one who perseveres under
trial because, having stood the test, that
person will receive the crown of life that*

the Lord has promised to those who love him.

Father, I pray you would give me strength to persevere in seeking you. Help me to spend more time in prayer for my family, for my church and the lost. Holy Spirit, I ask that you would direct my thoughts to whatever you wish me to pray for.

Open my eyes to the work you put in front of me, and help me give my all in fulfilling that work.

Father I ask you would expand my mind and understanding. Let my view of you become bigger and bigger so I might see more of your unending glory. Revive my heart. Let it burn fiercely for you. Let me see your holiness, so that I might worship you in Spirit and in truth.

Take my life, O God, and use it in your service. Whatever your will, let it be done.

In Jesus name, amen.

Further reading - Ephesians 1:15-23 / Hebrews 12

Take my life

Hebrews 10:19-25

Therefore, brothers and sisters, since we have confidence to enter the Most Holy Place by the blood of Jesus, by a new and living way opened for us through the curtain, that is, his body, and since we have a great priest over the house of God, let us draw near to God with a sincere heart and with the full assurance that faith brings, having our hearts sprinkled to cleanse us from a guilty conscience and having our bodies washed with pure water.

Let us hold unswervingly to the hope we profess, for he who promised is faithful. And let us consider how we may spur one another on toward love and good deeds, not giving up meeting together, as some are in the habit of doing, but encouraging one another — and all the more as you see the Day approaching.

Take my life and let it be
Consecrated, Lord, to thee.
Take my moments and my days,
let them flow in ceaseless praise.

Take my hands, and let them move
At the impulse of Thy love;
Take my feet, and let them be
Swift and beautiful for Thee.

Take my voice and let me sing
Always, only, for my King;
Take my lips and let them be
Filled with messages from Thee

Take my silver and my gold;
Not a mite would I withhold;
Take my intellect, and use
Every power as Thou shalt choose.

Take my will and make it Thine,
It shall be no longer mine:
Take my heart, it is Thine own;
It shall be Thy royal throne

Take my life; my Lord, I pour
At Thy feet its treasure-store;
Take myself, and I will be
Ever, only, all for Thee

Frances Ridley Havergal

Further reading - 2 Corinthians 6 / Galatians 2

We are all the work of your hand

Isaiah 64:1-8

Oh, that you would rend the heavens and come down, that the mountains would tremble before you! As when fire sets twigs ablaze and causes water to boil, come down to make your name known to your enemies and cause the nations to quake before you!

For when you did awesome things that we did not expect, you came down, and the mountains trembled before you.

Since ancient times no one has heard, no ear has perceived, no eye has seen any God besides you, who acts on behalf of those who wait for him.

You come to the help of those who gladly do right, who remember your ways. But when we continued to sin against them, you were angry. How then can we be saved?

All of us have become like one who is unclean, and all our righteous acts are like filthy rags; we all shrivel up like a leaf, and like the wind our sins sweep us away.

No one calls on your name or strives to lay hold of you; for you have hidden your face from us and have given us over to our sins.

Yet you, Lord, are our Father. We are the clay, you are the potter; we are all the work of your hand.

O Lord, you are merciful and gracious, slow to anger, abounding in steadfast love and faithfulness; keeping steadfast love for thousands, forgiving iniquity and transgression and sin.

What holiness! What might! May your name be lifted up in all the earth!

Let your kingdom come, and your will be done on earth as it is done in heaven. Let your kingdom come into my city. Let your word go out to save. O Lord, I ask for workers who will go out, to share the news of your great mercy. Let every knee bow, and every tongue confess that Jesus Christ is Lord.

Father, I bow before you. Humble my heart. Let no shadow of pride remain. Grant that I might be moulded into the image of your beloved Son. Help me to submit to every circumstance you bring me into, always trusting that you are sovereign. Let your will, and your will alone be done.

Forgive my rebellious heart, for I often choose my own way above yours. Grant me wisdom to know when I am doing this, and to immediately turn to you, with a repentant heart. Let me not continue in sin.

You are faithful to forgive, O Lord. We are so undeserving of your mercy, yet you extend it towards us again and again. The work of your Son on the cross is ever before me. Such incomprehensible love. Who is there like you?

There is no-one.

O Lord, let your name be lifted up in my life. Let me honour it always, I ask in Jesus name, amen.

Further reading - Psalm 73:23-28 / Psalm 63:1-8

His compassion never fails

Lamentations 3:22-26

Because of the Lord's great love we are not consumed, for his compassions never fail. They are new every morning; great is your faithfulness.

I say to myself, "The Lord is my portion; therefore I will wait for him." The Lord is good to those whose hope is in him, to the one who seeks him; it is good to wait quietly for the salvation of the Lord.

Lord God, thank you for this gift of a new day. Grant that I might grow in grace and increase in knowledge. Help me to know you as you truly are. Lord draw me close to you, and let love for you reign in my heart. O Father, I wish I could express how I feel about you. Words feel so clumsy, and inadequate when it comes to trying to put my heart before you.

By your grace, let my will respond to you. In myself, I know I have no power to obey you, and walk in your paths. Your love alone lifts me up, and enables me to walk according to your word. Your precious Spirit, dwelling in me, gives me strength and guidance, leading me in everything that pleases you.

Lord, lead me and guide me today. Let me respond in obedience to your every word. Grant me a humble heart, so that your glory shines through my life. There is no other purpose for me, except you. You are my heart, my strength and my song. Let your name be lifted up among your people, O God. I ask in Jesus name, amen.

Further reading - 1 Corinthians 1:18-31 / Acts 2:42-47

Be strong in the Lord

Eph 6:10-17

Finally, be strong in the Lord and in his mighty power. Put on the full armor of God, so that you can take your stand against the devil's schemes.

For our struggle is not against flesh and blood, but against the rulers, against the authorities, against the powers of this dark world and against the spiritual forces of evil in the heavenly realms.

Therefore put on the full armor of God, so that when the day of evil comes, you may be able to stand your ground, and after you have done everything, to stand.

Stand firm then, with the belt of truth buckled around your waist, with the breastplate of righteousness in place, and with your feet fitted with the readiness that comes from the gospel of peace.

In addition to all this, take up the shield of faith, with which you can extinguish

all the flaming arrows of the evil one.
Take the helmet of salvation and the
sword of the Spirit, which is the word of
God.

Lord God, you are my delight and song. At your throne I find a fountain of goodness and grace. Here I find mercy in my time of need, and the joy of your pleasure upon my life. Blessed be your holy name. For you reconciled me to yourself by the precious blood of your Son Jesus. Let this always be my most treasured thought.

Quicken my heart, O holy God. Fill me with holy zeal. Strengthen me that I might cling to you and never let you go. Thank you for your indescribable goodness towards me.

You have given me everything I need to walk according to your Word. Thank you for the life-giving truth of your Word. It exposes everything for what it truly is.

Thank you for the righteousness of Christ that you have poured upon me, and for His shed blood, by which I can come before you without dread.

Thank you for giving me living faith. I can truly trust in you with all my heart, and lean not on my own understanding.

Thank you that you have taken out my heart of stone, and given me a heart of flesh. You have given me eyes that see, and ears that hear.

I ask that you would ever expose the works of the evil one, so I would not be deceived. Let the glory of the work of the cross be ever on my mind.

As I read your word, I ask you would continue to protect me and draw me close to you. I ask this in the name of Jesus, amen.

Further reading - Psalm 103 / John 7:37-39

Holy, holy, holy is the Lord Almighty

Isaiah 6:1-4

In the year that King Uzziah died, I saw the Lord, high and exalted, seated on a throne; and the train of his robe filled the temple. Above him were seraphim, each with six wings: With two wings they covered their faces, with two they covered their feet, and with two they were flying. And they were calling to one another:

"Holy, holy, holy is the Lord Almighty; the whole earth is full of his glory."

At the sound of their voices the door-posts and thresholds shook and the temple was filled with smoke.

O King of glory, what majesty surrounds you. Your name is high above every name, and your goodness knows no bounds. You are from everlasting to everlasting, perfect in all your ways. Your splendour fills the heavens, and the earth is full of your praise. In you alone is life.

Lift up the hearts of your people to declare your Name. Teach us your ways, so we might walk in truth.

You are our strength and shield. Who else can we trust, but you? Who else can we turn to for help, but you? For you are strong and mighty. You rule over all, and you ordain every one of our days. You know the end from the beginning. In you alone is security and peace.

You sit enthroned in heaven. King of kings, and Lord of Lords. Grant strength to your people, and bless us with peace. In Jesus name, amen.

Further reading - Revelation 19:6-16 / Psalm 19

What's next?

You've reached the end of, *Daily Prayer Pursuing Holiness.* So now what?

How about reading through one of the shorter letters of Paul?

Do what I have done in this book. Take a few verses, think about them, and then base your prayers on what you have read. Perhaps even use a notebook to write them down.

Or, you might like to pray through another book in this series:

- Daily Prayer Seeking the Heart of God

- Daily Prayer Thru the Life of Jesus (Praying thru the Gospel of Luke)

- Daily Prayer Taking up the Shield of Faith (Praying thru Ephesians)

- Daily Prayer Drawing Near the Throne of Grace (Praying thru Hebrews)

=> To find this series, search on Amazon for Berenice Aguilera

Recently, I released a series of Bible journals. These are available in several different covers.

Each book covers an entire New Testament letter.

I have divided up the letters into easy Scripture portions for you to:

a) Write out,

b) Reflect on, or study further (it's up to you), and

c) A page to write a prayer based on the scripture and what you have learned.

If you are someone who likes to write out scripture verses, or Bible study notes, or wants help in the discipline of daily reading and study, these journals are perfect for you!

=> To find these journals, search Amazon for Berenice Aguilera Journals.

May our wonderful Lord bless you as you seek to love and serve Him.

BLACK JOURNAL FOR WOMEN

BLACK JOURNAL FOR MEN

ORANGE FLOWER SERIES

PARCHMENT SERIES

Each journal series is available for the following
books of the Bible:

- Galatians
- Ephesians
- Philippians
- Colossians
- 1 & 2 Thessalonians
- 1 & 2 Timothy, Titus, Philemon
- James
- 1 & 2 Peter
- 1, 2, 3 John, Jude

Printed in Great Britain
by Amazon

70456989R00047